What would
—See pag

Why did Dorothy get lost in Oz?
—See page 25

~

Why does a rooster crow?
—See page 35

~

What does "Macho" really mean?
—See page 77

~

What Olympic events would men always dominate?
—See page 115

How Are
MEN
~ Like ~
NOODLES?
2

The
Ultimate Jokebook
About Men

CINDY GARNER
Newport House, Inc.

Newport House, Inc.
1O7 R.R. 62O S., Suite 7-A
Austin, TX 78734

How are Men Like Noodles? 2 / Cindy Garner
First Newport House edition, 1992

Designed and typeset by Barbara Jezek

Manufactured in the United States of America

ISBN O-939515-15-6

More Humor Books from Newport House

How are Men Like Noodles?
Everything Men Know about Women
Sex after 60
77 Uses for an Ex
MEN! The Cartoon Book

**Thanks to these writers and friends
for their contributions:**

Rebecca Rhyne, Angela Ross, John Moore,
Karen Scullen, Bruce Kafaroff,
Kathy Borne, Joan Ambrose, Florence Small,
Linda Perret, Paul Seaburn, R. Stradtner,
Brian Morton, R. Dickert, Ron Ahlrich,
Edie Schiffendecker, Will Teed, Ben Green,
R. Livingston, M. Hartman, S. Cox,
R. Regent, Kent Graham, L. D'Oria,
D. Gephart, Judy Varon, Karen Dickson,
Pam L., Theresa Frohman, Bev Hershfield,
Margie Kelly, Leanna Wolfe, P. Miller,
Myra Moskowitz, Marion Moskowitz
Brenda Branch, C. Williams, Sally Egan,
Lora Cain, Nerby Jones, J. Anderson,
N. Ledwidge, Barbara Jezek, Eric Chunn,
Lillie Turney, Yolanda Lake, Carolyn Deeg,
Sandy Palmer, Donna Kress,
Ray Bard, and Rudy from UPS

To Margie Kelley, who always
laughs at my jokes

CONTENTS

IF WOMEN
RAN THINGS

Mother's Day would become Mother's Week.

~

Panty hose would be tax deductable.

~

Football season would be one week long.

~

Fashion shows would pre-empt baseball games.

Male graduates would be told, "Sorry, the only opening we have is for a secretary."

~

Men would have to shave their legs and underarms.

~

Asking for directions would become a sign of manliness.

~

Gossip would be considered "Female Bonding."

~

There would be a littering fine for dropping dirty clothes on the floor.

~

After a divorce, men would have trouble getting credit in their own names.

New felonies:
Not phoning home
Burping
Body odor
Beer breath
Leaving the toilet seat up

~

Men would automatically be expected to
make coffee for their female bosses.

~

The Secretary of Defense would be either
Thelma or Louise.

~

Men would have to wear high heels.

~

Women in childbirth would get combat pay.

~

Women would read at the breakfast table
while men tried to make conversation.

Women would say to their husbands, "I don't know why you can't run the household on the money I give you."

~

There'd be a 7 day waiting period before men could purchase remote controls.

~

Female executives would say to one another, "Let's do lunch. Have your boy call my boy."

~

Older women would be described as "distinguished," while older men would just be called "old."

~

ROMANCE

Men promise us women wine and poetry if we marry them. What do we usually get?

   Beer and television.

~

Why do men like "love at first sight"?

   It saves them a lot of time.

~

What do men consider most important in selecting the perfect place for dining out?

a. a maitre d' for good service
b. exquisite food
c. a big screen TV and plenty of cold beer

~

You're sitting on the sofa with your man. You turn out the light. Does he:

a. Pretend nothing has happened?
b. Get romantic?
c. Take the hint and go home?

~

What question comes up most when a man takes his woman out for dinner?

"Would you like fries with that?"

~

MEN AND WOMEN

A woman of 35 thinks of having children.
What does a man of 35 think of?

Dating children.

~

How can you tell soap operas are fictional?

In real life, men aren't affectionate out
of bed.

~

Where can a woman hide her diary so her
husband will never find it?

a. the dishwasher
b. the laundry room
c. her side of the bed

~

What qualities do most men look for in a woman?

Depends on whether it's 2 p.m. or 2 a.m.

~

String bikinis cut off circulation to:

a. women's arms
b. women's legs
c. men's brains

~

How are men and women similar when it comes to looks?

Women care about how they look, and men care about how women look.

~

ONE UP ON MEN

Why is our country in such a mess today?

   Because there aren't enough female politicians to clean up the messes that male politicians make.

~

What should you give a man who has everything?

   A woman to show him how to work it.

Men think we don't know half the things
they're up to. What's really the only thing
they can do behind our backs?

Zip us up.

~

What's the difference between male bonding
and female bonding?

Female bonding doesn't require anyone to
get knee-crawling drunk.

~

In modern times women can now live their
dreams to be astronauts, senators and
doctors. How can men live their dreams?

By watching the ESPN sports channel 24
hours a day.

~

Why does a man get more exercise dressing
than a woman?

A man has to bend over to pick up his
clothes off the floor.

Why did God make man before woman?

    She was practicing.

~

What's the difference between how a man
and a women decorate a room?

    She asks herself what color looks best. He
asks himself what color hides dirt best.

~

MEN

What do men consider the four seasons?

Football, basketball, baseball, and hockey.

~

Why did Dorothy get lost in Oz?

She had 3 men giving her directions.

~

Why do black widow spiders kill their males after mating?

To stop the snoring before it starts.

What is the difference between the average man and a circus clown?

A circus clown wears funny looking clothes on purpose.

~

A man thinks he is a snappy dresser. What does this probably mean?

His socks match each other.

~

What is the difference between a man and a Ginsu knife?

The Ginsu knife isn't always worried about whether it can still "cut it."

~

How can you tell "It's a man's world"?

a. Everything is so logical and orderly.
b. Working women are always fairly paid.
c. Women couldn't possibly have done as well.
d. None of the above.

Your man has just bought a satellite dish and a new 48 inch color television set. What can you be sure of?

The remote control will get more action than you.

~

What is the best way to make sure that your man doesn't make a fool of himself at a party?

Leave him at home.

~

What can you say about those guys at the health club who parade around showing off their perfect builds?

They're unemployed.

~

Why do men have "ring around the collar"?

It comes from the ring around their necks!

Why is it no use telling a man to go to hell?

He'd just get lost on the way.

~

When a man says he prefers you in a "natural" look, what does he mean?

He means he wants to see you naked.

~

What's the best way to get a man out of the house?

Tell him your mother's coming over.

~

Why don't men have mid-life crises?

They stay stuck in adolescence.

~

What do men and pantyhose have in common?

They cling to women, but one rough spot and watch them run!

Why do men always use the express lanes at grocery stores?

They can only remember 7 items.

~

How does a man show he's planning for the future?

He buys two cases of beer instead of one.

~

WHAT ARE
MEN LIKE?

How are men like babies?

They make a fuss when you try to change them.

~

How are men like bread?

They're easier to take when you butter them up.

~

Why are men like vending machines?

They take your money, but half the time they won't work.

~

How are men like air bags?

They only open up under pressure.

~

How are wonderful men like atoms?

You've heard they exist, but you've yet to actually see one.

~

How are most men like modern art?

Hard to understand and not really worth the effort.

~

Why are men like bracelets?

Outside of occasionally looking good on your arm, neither serves any other useful purpose whatsoever.

How are men like soap?

When they get in hot water, they disappear.

~

How is a man like the Defense Department?

Each is deceptive, wasteful, and claims to act in your best interests.

~

HABITS

Why does a rooster crow?

   Being a typical male, he's trying to take credit for the eggs the hens lay.

~

Why were they called "The Dark Ages"?

   No man thought of reading the directions to find out how to turn on the lights.

~

How do you know if a man's happy?

See if he has a beer in one hand and a remote control in the other.

~

You've been gone for a week and your husband is responsible for keeping house. You will find . . .

a. a sink full of dirty dishes
b. a hamper full of dirty clothes
c. an empty refrigerator
d. all of the above

~

Some men will drive around and around the block to look for parking. This is caused by:

a. their hunter instinct
b. their sincere belief that there's a space out there that's "meant" for them
c. they're too cheap to pay $1 for parking

~

What's a man's idea of "quality time"?

Talking to his kids during a commercial.

How can you tell if a man is tired when he comes home from work?

He can barely hold his beer can up.

~

What's a man's ideas of good manners?

Waiting between courses to belch.

~

While driving, when does a man know to speed up?

When someone tries to pass him.

~

NEATNESS

How will other life forms know that men have been to the moon?

   They left stuff littered all over the place.

~

What's a man's idea of helping out around the house?

   Dropping his clothes where it's easy for you to pick them up.

~

How can you tell if a man has lived alone long enough?

He considers the green thing growing in his refrigerator a pet.

~

Why is it wrong to call men pigs?

It's an insult to millions of hardworking livestock.

~

Why do men need only 4 pairs of underwear?

One each for summer, fall, winter, and spring.

~

How can you tell when your man has cleaned the bathroom?

The bathtub ring is smeared.

~

Why should hurricanes be named only after men?

They mess up everything and expect someone else to clean it up.

What's the only recycling most men do?

They use their beer cans as ash trays before throwing them away.

~

I think the Men's Movement is a great idea. I just wish part of the movement they made was to pick up their clothes.

~

What's the difference between a bachelor's bathroom and a toxic dump?

The dump might actually get cleaned by the EPA one day.

~

MEN'S OPINIONS

What do men consider the four basic food groups?

Beer, chips, dip, and hamburger.

~

A man says that he has just seen a really magnificent work of art. What is he probably describing?

a. A painting by a great artist like Rembrandt
b. His secretary in a tight sweater

Men always pretend they know everything. When a man gives an opinion, how much is it usually really worth?

  a. $5
  b. 50c
  c. Let's just say that when he asks to add his 2c worth, he isn't overcharging.

~

Why are men wrong to explain away their losses by saying, "That's just the way the ball bounces"?

  Because they're usually the one who dropped it!

~

What do men consider "female" problems?

  The dishwasher and vacuum being broke.

~

What's a man's idea of a personal growth experience?

Watching a "Monster Truck and Tractor Pull."

~

What's a man's idea of male bonding?

Bailing his best friend out of jail.

~

When a man starts thinking deep thoughts, what questions does he ask himself:

a. Does God exist?
b. What is the meaning of life?
c. Why couldn't the professor have invented something to get Gilligan and his friends off the island?

~

How can you make a man concerned about the environment?

Tell him there could be a global beer shortage.

~

MEN IN HISTORY

Why did the Emperor have no clothes?

His wife had been out of town for a week.

~

Why did Moses spend 40 years wandering in the desert?

He refused to ask for directions.

~

How was Adam a typical male?

The first time something went wrong, he blamed Eve.

Why did Washington spend that fateful frozen Christmas with his troops?

His wife asked him to help clean up the house for the holidays.

~

How was Colonel Sanders a typical male?

All he cared about were legs, breasts, and thighs.

~

BACHELORS

How do you scare a bachelor?

Sneak up behind him and start throwing rice.

~

How can you tell a bachelor's not a big spender?

He sends a glass of water over to your table.

~

How is being at a singles bar different from going to the circus?

At the circus, the clowns don't talk.

~

What makes men chase women they have no intention of marrying?

The same urge that makes dogs chase cars they have no intention of driving.

~

What food describes most bachelors?

Jerky.

~

Men will brag that there are women waiting by the phone at this very moment for their call. Who are they?

Women working at 900 numbers!

~

How is a bachelor like a used car?

Both are easy to get, cheap, and unreliable.

Where is the best place in a book store to find a man who is handsome, a good lover, and a stimulating partner?

In the pages of a romance novel.

~

What do you do with a bachelor who thinks he's God's gift?

Exchange him.

~

Why is the book **Women Who Love too Much** a disappointment for many men?

No phone numbers.

~

What's a man's idea of a perfect date?

A woman who answers the door stark naked holding a 6 pack.

A man who says he "practically lives in the kitchen," most likely . . .

    a. is a gourmet cook
    b. appreciates fine food
    c. lives in an efficiency apartment

~

Why do bachelors like smart women?

    Opposites attract.

~

**What a Bachelor Says
(and the Truth)**

I have a place at the beach."
(he's renting a tent for the weekend)

"I've had several leadership positions."
(in the Cub Scouts)

"My company is thinking of transferring me."
(to the unemployment line)

"I have a position in oil exploration."
(He checks dipsticks at the filling station.)

"My salary is into six figures."
(if you count cents)

"I keep my funds in a diversified portfolio."
($2O cash, $2O checking, $2O savings)

"My wife and I were incompatible."
(She threw me out.)

"I'd like to teach you about geology."
(Yeah, I'd like to have the two of us make the earth move!)

"I feel beauty is only skin deep."
(which is deep enough for me)

"I enjoy the theater."
(rated XXX)

"I feel something special for you."
(Lust.)

"I want to know all about you."
(in 2 minutes or less)

What His Personal Ad Says
(and the Truth)

"Looking for a woman to share the rest of my life with."
(He wants a one-night stand and he's willing to lie in order to get it.)

"I want a woman who will be there for me in good times and in bad times."
(He wants someone to sleep with who will also clean.)

"I like women and enjoy their company."
(He dates thirty or forty women at the same time.)

QUIZ #1

Rating a Man's Potential as a Date

Circle the answers that apply.

1. Where you met

    a. symphony fund raiser
    b. through friends
    c. you walked past a construction site and
       he whistled

2. His income

    a. six figures
    b. executive level
    c. wants to find a woman to support him

3. Favorite topic of conversation

    a. conversant on almost any subject
    b. sports
    c. himself

4. Marital status

    a. single
    b. divorced
    c. married but pretending to be single

5. His fragrance

    a. Dior cologne
    b. Aqua Velva
    c. beer

Score the quiz as follows:

3 points for each "a" answer
2 points for each "b" answer
1 points for each "c" answer

Scoring key:

11-15   Excellent dating material
6-10   If he's the only one available
0-5   Stay home and watch TV

MARRIAGE

How can you tell if a new husband is cheap?

At the wedding, he brings a catcher's mitt to catch the rice.

~

How else can you tell if a new husband is cheap?

He asks the minister for separate checks.

~

How can you tell if a new husband has a big ego?

He orders a wedding cake with only a statue of him.

~

Why do men like to marry women who remind them of their mothers?

Who else would put up with them?

~

How would marrying a divorced man be like buying a used car?

You should be able to speak to the previous owner and find out why she got rid of it.

~

When a man gets married, he . . .

    a. pledges his love for eternity
    b. starts thinking in terms of "two" instead of just "one"
    c. stops depending on his mom and starts depending on his wife

~

WHY MEN MARRY

The top 10 reasons why men get married:

10. Their mothers refuse to do their laundry anymore

9. Their tax accountants recommend it.

8. They need someone to clean up their mess.

7. They need someone to install the batteries in their remote control.

6. They run out of food.

5. Sex.

4. Sex.

3. Sex.

2. Sex.

1. Sex.

~

HUSBANDS

How are husbands like cats?

   Never around when you want them, but always back for dinner.

~

What does a husband consider a luxury?

   Anything his wife needs.

~

What is the difference between a man on a date and a man who is married?

On a date a man will wine and dine you. A man who is married just whines.

~

Why do men have a harder time dealing with their parents than their wives?

They feel guilty lying to their parents.

~

When women say their husband is "well-rounded," they're talking about his . . .

a. education
b. interests
c. waistline

~

You're spending a quiet evening at home alone with your husband. He most wants . . .

a. to talk
b. to make love
c. to have the remote control

What do a husband and a parrot have in common?

Neither one has anything new to say.

~

How is a husband like a car?

a. They both have a spare tire.
b. They both have deadly exhaust.
c. When you need them the most, they're usually in the garage.

~

Why are husbands like lawn mowers?

They're hard to get started, emit foul odors, and don't work half the time.

~

After they're married, most men stop seeing . . .

a. their old bachelor buddies
b. their old girlfriends
c. their feet when they stand up

How are husbands like workout clothes?

They're both too tight.

~

When does a husband think he's getting better at sex?

When he gets it down to under 30 seconds.

~

A married man opening the car door for a lady is a sign . . .

a. of good breeding
b. of proper etiquette
c. that he's not with his wife

~

Why are banks better than husbands?

They pay you more interest.

~

How can you tell if your husband is lazy?

He hears that career and marriage don't mix, so he quits his job.

~

You've prepared your husband's favorite dinner. Afterwards, he will . . .

    a. thank you with a kiss
    b. help with the dishes
    c. burp

~

How is a longtime husband like an old dog?

    Neither one knows any new tricks.

~

Your husband's best friend joined a gym, lost weight, and looks great. Because of this, your husband will . . .

    a. join a gym and lose weight also
    b. talk about getting some exercise
    c. get a new best friend

To most men, their wedding ring is . . .

    a. a symbol of unending love
    b. a sign of their commitment
    c. the first thing that comes off at the
       "singles bar"

~

WHAT ARE HUSBANDS LIKE?

How is a husband like the Larry King Show?

They're both "all talk."

~

How is a husband like an old car?

All the equipment's there, but you never know when it's gonna work.

~

How is a husband like the painting that Aunt Mabel gave you?

When people come to visit, you'd like to hide both of them.

~

How is a husband like a cat?

Neither one will follow directions.

~

FAITHFULNESS

What word best describes most men in singles bars?

Married.

~

What's a man's favorite weather report?

"The coast is clear!"

~

What do a husband and a cockroach have in common?

They're both always sneaking around.

Why do men prefer to go out with blonds?

It's difficult to detect blond hairs on
a white T- shirt.

~

Why is dog man's best friend?

It won't tell on him.

~

If a husband catches his wife in bed with
another man, he calls it adultery. If his wife
catches him in bed with another woman, what
does he call it?

Flirting.

~

To most men, "monogamy" means . . .

    a. having only one wife
    b. having sexual relations with only one
       person
    c. all his girlfriends should only have sex
       with him

Why do many men prefer the lights on during sex?

That way they're less likely to say the wrong name.

~

HANDY-MEN

What does a man consider "doing his share" around the house?

Remembering to put down the toilet seat.

~

What is the best way to get your man to take out the garbage?

a. Tell him it stinks.
b. Remind him he promised to do it yesterday.
c. Threaten him.
d. Tell him the woman next door is sun bathing.

A man who claims he can do "2 things at once" most likely . . .

a. simultaneously uses both sides of his brain
b. has exceptional organizational skills
c. counts "breathing" as one of them

~

Nine times out of 10, a man holding a mop is . . .

a. helping his wife clean the house
b. taking care of something he just spilled
c. a mop salesman

~

What does the average man do about a leaky faucet?

a. He fixes it.
b. He calls a plumber in to fix it.
c. He has a beer and pretends he doesn't hear it.

What's a man's idea of helping with the baby?

Telling his wife when the diaper needs changing.

~

HELPFULNESS

What does "Macho" really mean?

"Men Avoiding Chores at Home and Outside"

~

What's a man's idea of helping to make a bed?

Getting up out of it.

~

When does a fellow give you the shirt off his back?

When he wants you to do his laundry.

How do men do their part to conserve energy?

They come home and do nothing.

~

What's the greatest contradiction about husbands?

How they can't take the time to pick up their socks, but have time to hand wash and wax their cars.

~

What does a wife have to do to get a few minutes to herself?

Do the dishes.

~

When do men prefer their coffee black?

When there's no one around to get them the cream from the fridge.

~

ATTENTIVENESS

What's a husband's idea of "being polite"?

Dancing with every other women in the room—except his wife.

~

A man is never more witty or charming than when he's . . .

a. out with you for a romantic evening
b. meeting your parents for the first time
c. talking to the sales girl at Victoria's Secret

You just spent $100 at the most exclusive hair salon in town. If you ask your man, "Notice anything different?", what's his most likely reply?

"Is that a new dress?"

~

Men never listen to women. Why is it men can hear the price of power tools being marked down at a discount store 5 miles away, but they can't hear us say, "What do you want for dinner?"

~

What's a man's idea of being attentive during sex?

Turning off the TV.

~

How does marriage change men sexually?

They go from tri-weekly to try weakly.

~

WOMEN

Why is the Wizard of Oz's Dorothy a good candidate for marriage?

   She's used to hanging around with men who have no courage, no heart, and no brains.

~

Why did Snow White eat the poison apple?

   Wouldn't you if you had to clean up after seven men?

~

Why would a woman find it unbearable to be married to a man with multiple personalities?

She would have to listen to 20 different excuses for why he came home late from work.

~

What lesson does living with men teach women?

That sometimes, nothing is better than something.

~

Why should a woman be relieved when her man burps in public?

It could have come out the other end.

~

How can a woman make her home 90% fat free?

Throw her husband out.

~

NO GOOD MEN

Which highway sign is always wrong?

"Men at Work"

~

In a typical office, why do the men hold so many meetings?

It's their way of passing the time while they're waiting for the woman on the staff to get the work done.

~

If life is a highway, what are men?

Speed bumps.

I can't understand why men go bald. You'd think hair would grow great on top of 200 pounds of pure fertilizer!

~

What's the worst advice a counselor can give most men?

Be yourself.

~

What did God say after he created man?

"I knew I should have hired a quality control supervisor."

~

Why are men reluctant to become fathers?

They aren't through being children.

~

What country-western song best describes men?

a. "Your Cheatin' Heart"

b. "Everything You Touch Turns to Dirt"
c. "You are Just Another Sticky Wheel on the Grocery Cart of Life"

~

What title for a self-help book would summarize the truth about men?

Men Who Love Themselves Too Much

~

Men don't need a physical fitness program. They get enough exercise

a. jumping to conclusions
b. flying off the handle
c. pushing their luck
d. dodging responsibility

~

What is the difference between a man and a pack of cigarettes?

Both of them can make you sick, but at least the cigarettes come with a warning.

~

How was Christopher Columbus a typical man?

He thought he knew where he was going, but he was lost.

~

What do men think paternity leave is?

Getting out of town before the girl's father finds out.

~

How is a man like Communism?

Neither one works.

~

How many men does it take to screw in a light bulb?

None. Every man knows that if he puts off changing the bulb long enough, a woman will take care of it.

~

What's a man's definition of manners?

Saying "Excuse me" after burping.

~

MY GUY

My guy always tells people he's a CPA. In his case, it means Car Parking Attendant.

~

My guy says his fears about the nation's employment problems are over. For a while there, he was scared someone was going to offer him a job.

~

My guy is so lazy, when he broke his arm, our family doctor saw no reason to put it in a cast.

Last night, my guy whispered those 3 little words that he has been whispering to me ever since our love affair began . . . "Is dinner ready?"

~

They say that Madonna has sex 10 to 12 times a week. My guy doesn't *speak* to me that many times in a week.

~

Last night, my guy satisfied me again . . . He slept in the guest bedroom.

~

I told my husband I wanted a hot night and to be held close. So he bought me an electric blanket and a girdle.

~

QUIZ #2

Rating Your Man's Romantic Potential

Circle the answers that apply.

1. Your man's idea of a pleasant evening

   a. candlelight, a fine dinner, and a vintage
      wine
   b. eating out and going to a movie
   c. getting drunk with the boys

2. You say, "I love you." He says

   a. "Darling, I love you too!"

b. "That's nice, dear."
c. "Look, an interception!"

3. Your man's choice for a romantic vacation

    a. Rio
    b. Paris
    c. Motel 6

4. His idea of entertainment

    a. Ballet
    b. Pops concert
    c. Bar hopping

5. What he says when he's in a romantic mood

    a. "I love you madly, passionately."
    b. "I yearn for you when you are gone."
    c. "How about a roll in the hay?"

Score the quiz as follows:

3 points for each "a" answer
2 points for each "b" answer
1 points for each "c" answer

Scoring key:

11-15   Very romantic. Keep your eye on him.
6-1O   Above average romantic.
O-5   Split a six pack with him.

MEN AND MONEY

What's the difference between men and money?

    Money talks.

~

What is a man's idea of bringing home the bacon?

    Renting Porky Pig videos.

~

How can you tell if a man believes in free speech?

He uses your phone to call his friends in other states.

~

When a man says he's "raking it in," he most likely . . .

    a. has a very lucrative job
    b. has made some sound investments
    c. has a job mowing lawns

~

How can you tell if a man is ahead of his time?

He's already spent his next paycheck.

~

How can you tell if a man you meet in church is cheap?

He gives the Lord credit—but no cash.

How can you tell if your man is cheap?

He puts off buying the World Book Encyclopedia for your child until it comes out in paperback.

~

How else can you tell if your man is cheap?

His favorite saying is "The best things in life are free."

~

MEN AND ANIMALS

What is the difference between your man and the dog eating in the next room?

The dog doesn't burp.

~

How is a dog like a man?

The dog doesn't like to take a bath, has no table manners, and likes to scratch in embarrassing places.

How are men like fish?

All the fun is in the catching.

~

Why do scientists prefer laboratory mice over men?

You can train lab mice.

~

What's the difference between a new husband and a new dog?

After a year, the dog is still excited to see you.

~

MEN AND FOOD

What's a man's idea of a good cut of meat?

Hamburger.

~

How are men like delicatessens?

They're both full of baloney.

~

What would men consider a health food breakthrough?

Oat bran beer.

How are men like eggs?

They're both scrambled.

~

Complete this sentence:

Where there's smoke there _____.

  a. fire
  b. a man cooking

~

How can you tell if a man is religious?

When he cooks, take a look at the burnt offerings he serves you.

~

What's the greatest mystery about a man?

How he can get every pot and pan in the place dirty just fixing franks and beans.

What's a major conflict of interest for men?

When pizza arrives during sex.

~

Why don't men like wine?

Too hard to work up a burp.

~

SEX

What's the closest thing to sex a married woman has?

Exercising with her "Thighmaster."

~

How is marital sex like the election of a Democratic president?

It doesn't happen very often.

~

How do you know if a man's sexually satisfied?

See if he's snoring.

~

Why is sleeping with a man like a soap opera?

Just when it's getting interesting, they're finished until next time.

~

A man who doesn't want sex after buying an expensive dinner probably . . .

a. wants to show that his intentions are
   more than physical
b. wants to wait until he knows you better
c. is your husband

~

What's the difference between a 6-pack and lovemaking?

A man can make a 6-pack last longer than 3 minutes.

~

How is a man different from a hot fudge sundae?

Hot fudge sundaes always satisfy a woman.

~

To most men, practicing "safe sex" means . . .

  a. using a condom
  b. being true to his woman
  c. meeting his mistress at least 20 miles
     away from where he lives

~

Why do men like waterbeds?

  During sex the bed does half the work.

~

How can you tell if a man's in the mood
for sex?

  Check his pulse.

~

What do men consider foreplay?

  Buying dinner.

What else do men consider foreplay?

Asking if you're in the mood.

~

How can you tell when a man's interest in sex
has waned?

The only itch he feels is jock itch.

~

How else can you tell if a man has lost
interest in sex?

He watches X-rated movies— for the story
line!

~

How can you tell if a man's a lousy lover?

Even his inflatable woman has headaches.

~

When a man says he can make love all night,
what does he really mean?

He can make love for 5 minutes and brag about it all night.

~

Why is "Phone Sex" popular with men?

Because when it comes to sex, most men are only talk anyway.

~

What can you say to a man who's just had sex?

Anything you like. He's asleep.

~

What food reminds women of their man's performance in bed?

Minute Rice.

~

COMMUNICATING

How is a man like call waiting?

Both constantly interrupt your conversations.

~

What do you call a man who wants to hear only about you every time you meet?

A psychologist.

~

What do men consider to be a long conversation?

One that lasts through 2 commercials.

~

If silence were golden, most women would be millionaires.

~

To most men, the words "I love you" are . . .

   a. a term of endearment
   b. an expression of deep affection
   c. foreplay

~

What's the non-verbal signal for "I'm listening" in men?

   Taking the remote control out of their hands and resting it on their stomachs.

~

When a man gets the last word, what should it be?

   "Yes."

Why do men find it difficult to make eye contact?

Breasts don't have eyes.

~

How do men make a long story short?

They interrupt.

~

SPORTS

Why do men like auto racing?

Because they can go as fast as they want without having to ask for directions.

~

Why do men like domed sports stadiums?

The rain doesn't get in their beer.

~

Is weight lifting good exercise for the average man?

Yes, especially if he starts by picking up his clothes from the floor!

~

How is a man playing baseball like a dog with fleas?

Neither is embarrassed to scratch where they itch.

~

At what time of the day do scientists say men are most attentive?

Halftime.

~

Why do men jog?

a. To keep in shape.
b. To avoid being hit by angry wives and girlfriends.

Olympic events men would always dominate:

1. Six- pack toss
2. Synchronized belching
3. Remote control dash
4. Dirty clothes toss
5. Marathon lying

What is the most common football injury?

A blister on the remote control thumb.

~

How can you tell that a man isn't sincere about getting fit?

He puts his exercise bike on cruise control.

~

CHANGING PLACES

How would things be different if men got cramps?

a. Drugstores would be stocked with "Midol in a Drum."
b. PMS would be a legitimate defense for murder.
c. The Secret Service would have to hide the panic button from the President on those really bad days.

~

What would happen if men had cramps?

There'd be a PMS telethon.

INTELLIGENCE

Three guys walking along the road spot a magic lantern. The first guy rubs the lantern and a genie comes out. The genie says, "You have three wishes, which comes out to one wish each. Choose your wish carefully.

The first guy asks to be 100 times smarter than he is now and the genie says, "Your wish is granted!"

The second guy asks to be 100 times smarter than the first guy. The genie says, "No problem!" and grants the wish.

The third guy thinks and thinks and finally asks to be 10,000 times smarter than the second guy. The genie says, "Are you *sure*? I mean, it would be a really big change."

The guy grows upset and insists he have his wish.

So the genie grants his wish and . . . turns him into a woman!

~

DIVORCE

What do you call a man who's just lost 90% of his brains?

Newly divorced.

~

I'm finally talking to my ex again. Just this morning, I told him to drop dead.

~

My marriage broke up because of illness. I got sick of him.

~

My therapist told me to get rid of the low priority things in my life . . . so I got a divorce.

BACKWARDS
JOKES

A: The unemployment lines.

Q: Where would the typical highly paid executive be if he didn't have a poorly paid woman secretary to do most of his work?

~

A: Superman.

Q: What do they call a man who has the intelligence, endurance, and ability of the average woman.

~

A: Dinner, bed, commitments.

Q: Name 3 things a man can't make.

~

A: A shopping cart with wobbly wheels, bags that break, and a husband.

Q: Name 3 things that are worthless in a grocery store.

~

A: Bethlehem.

Q: Where were the last 3 wise men?

~

A: Say anything.

Q: What do you have to do to find out why men are called "the opposite sex"?

~

A: *Everything Men Know about Women.*

Q: What's the name of a popular *blank* book?

A: "I have a headache," "It'll wake the kids," "I'm not in the mood."

Q: What are the most common excuses a man uses to get out of taking out the trash?

~

A: A frying pan, a broken household appliance, and a wife's G-spot.

Q: Name 3 things a husband never touches.

~

A: Men and microwave dinners.

Q: Name 2 things that are hot and ready in 2 minutes?

~

A: A marathon

Q: Where does a married woman have to go to hear heavy breathing?

A: Single.

Q: What do you call a man who opens car doors for women?

~

MORE LAUGHS!